The Illustrated Story of President

JOHN TAYLOR

Great Leaders of The Church
of Jesus Christ of Latter-day Saints

The Illustrated Story of President John Taylor
Great Leaders of The Church of Jesus Christ
of Latter-day Saints

Copyright © 1982 by
Eagle Systems International
P.O. Box 508
Provo, Utah 84603

ISBN: 0-938762-03-6
Library of Congress Catalog Card No.: 82-70690

Second Printing March 1983

First Edition

Lithographed in U.S.A.
by
COMMUNITY PRESS, INC.

A Member of
The American Bookseller's Association
New York, New York

The Illustrated Story of President

JOHN TAYLOR

Great Leaders of The Church of Jesus Christ of Latter-day Saints

AUTHOR
Della Mae Rasmussen

ILLUSTRATOR
B. Keith Christensen

DIRECTOR AND CORRELATOR
Lael J. Woodbury

ADVISORS AND EDITORS
Paul & Millie Cheesman
Mark Ray Davis
L. Norman Egan
Annette Hullinger
Beatrice W. Friel

PUBLISHER
Steven R. Shallenberger

A
Biography Of
JOHN TAYLOR

The favorite motto of President John Taylor was "The Kingdom of God or Nothing." He lived his whole life as an example of this belief.

John Taylor was the third President of The Church of Jesus Christ of Latter-day Saints. He was born in Milnthorpe, Westmoreland County, England, on November 1, 1808. He was an industrious young boy and learned anything to which he put his mind and effort very quickly. He had a vision early in his life that left him with the impression that God had something special for him to do on the earth. His vision proved to be prophetic.

John's family moved to Canada in 1830; two years later he joined them there. In 1833 he married Leonora Cannon. They studied the Bible together and became dissatisfied with the religions of the day. Parley P. Pratt came as a missionary to the area where the Taylors lived. Elder Pratt preached the true gospel of Jesus Christ and told them of the Prophet Joseph Smith and the Book of Mormon. John and Leonora Taylor soon recognized the truth of Brother Pratt's words and were baptized. When Elder Pratt finished his stay, he left John Taylor in charge of the Church affairs in Upper Canada. Joseph Smith visited John Taylor in Canada and soon thereafter sent a request for him to join the Saints in Missouri. John Taylor was ordained an apostle by Brigham Young and Heber C. Kimball at Far West, Missouri, on December 19, 1838. In 1839 he served a mission in England, the first of four missions for the Church.

When he returned from Great Britain, he took his family to live in Nauvoo. There he was an editor of the newspapers *Times and Seasons* and the *Nauvoo Neighbor*. He became one of the most capable and inspiring speakers and writers in the Church. He went with the Prophet Joseph Smith and his brother Hyrum Smith to Carthage Jail. When Joseph and Hyrum were murdered, John was severely wounded.

In 1847 John Taylor led a company of Saints from Winter Quarters to Salt Lake City. He was active in the territorial government and continued to use his unusually keen intellect and writing ability in the service of the Lord. He became known as the "Defender of the Faith" and the "Champion of Liberty."

John Taylor was sustained as President of the Council of the Twelve on October 6, 1877, and served for three years. He was sustained as President of the Church on October 10, 1880. In 1884 he was forced into exile because he had plural families. He continued to send written messages to his people and to exercise leadership of the Church. He was in exile for about two and one half years and died in Kaysville, Utah, on July 25, 1887, at the age of seventy-eight.

When he died, Elder Lorenzo Snow said of him: "The Latter-day Saints feel that they have lost a friend . . . that we have lost one of the greatest men that has stood upon the earth since the days of the Son of God—a man whose virtue, whose integrity, whose resolution to pursue the path of righteousness is known, and well known."

He was unsurpassed as a devoted servant of the Lord.

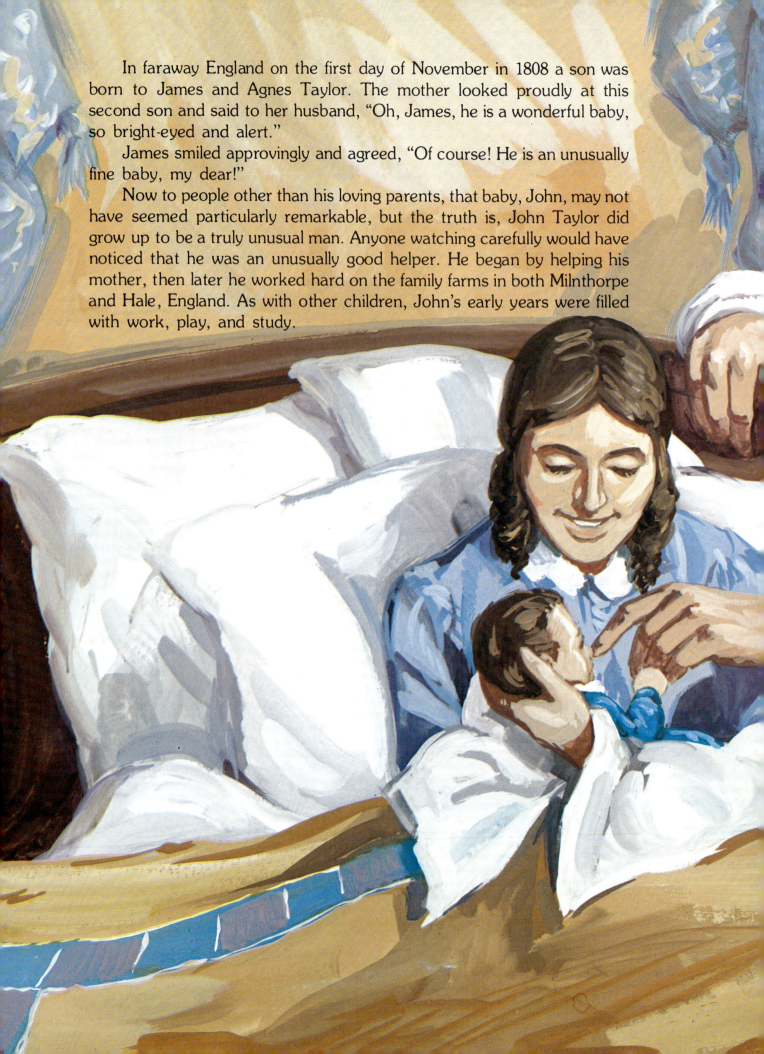

In faraway England on the first day of November in 1808 a son was born to James and Agnes Taylor. The mother looked proudly at this second son and said to her husband, "Oh, James, he is a wonderful baby, so bright-eyed and alert."

James smiled approvingly and agreed, "Of course! He is an unusually fine baby, my dear!"

Now to people other than his loving parents, that baby, John, may not have seemed particularly remarkable, but the truth is, John Taylor did grow up to be a truly unusual man. Anyone watching carefully would have noticed that he was an unusually good helper. He began by helping his mother, then later he worked hard on the family farms in both Milnthorpe and Hale, England. As with other children, John's early years were filled with work, play, and study.

Then one day his father said, "John, you are now fourteen years old. You will need a way to earn your livelihood. We must decide what trade you should learn."

John answered, "I know you are right, Father. It's hard for me to leave my family, but I know I must have a trade." Shortly after that John went away to Liverpool, where he became an apprentice to a barrel manufacturer. But within a few months the business failed, and he returned home.

"I am not discouraged," said young John. "I will look for another opportunity." This time he went to Penrith in Cumberland. As usual he worked hard and learned quickly. He became skilled in the art of woodworking, a skill he was to find useful all his life.

In addition to having unusual intelligence and working hard, John was exceptional in other ways. He was deeply religious. During his youth he and his family studied the Holy Bible, and he grew to have a strong faith in God. He was baptized as an infant into the Church of England. However, when he was sixteen years old, he joined the Methodist Church.

At about this time something very unusual happened to John, and it influenced him for the rest of his life. He had a vision! He said, "I saw an angel blowing a trumpet and proclaiming a heavenly message. I did not know what it was. But God must have something special for me to do."

One day in the year 1830 James and Agnes Taylor called their family together. They said, "We have decided to leave England and emigrate to Canada. We believe there will be more opportunity for us there." Then James Taylor turned to his son. "John," he said, "I have great trust in you. I am asking you to stay in England to settle our family affairs and to sell our property; then you will join us in Canada."

John replied, "I will do my best, Father."

After his family sailed off for Canada, John felt very lonely at times. It was two years before he was able to complete the business and join his family at their new home in Toronto, Canada. What rejoicing there was when the family was reunited once again! John was now twenty-four years old, and he lost no time in setting up a business as a woodturner.

John had never forgotten his vision. He felt a strong desire to preach the gospel, and because of this he became a teacher and traveling preacher for the church he had joined as a youth in England. While John was attending the meetings of this church, he met Leonora Cannon. She was refined, witty, educated, and as deeply religious as he was. John immediately saw that she was an exceptional young lady and soon fell in love with her. These two seemed perfectly matched. They married and set up housekeeping in Toronto.

John said to his new wife, "Leonora, let us join together with a few friends in a Bible study group. We must learn all we can about the scriptures." They did this, but a curious thing happened. The more John and Leonora studied the Bible, the more concerned they became. Finally John said to Leonora, "Certain doctrines taught by Jesus and the apostles are not taught by any of the religious sects. If the Bible is true, then the doctrines we have been taught are false. If the ones we have been taught are true, then the Bible is false."

Leonora suggested, "Let us fast and pray, and perhaps God will send us an answer."

John agreed and said, "We will pray that if the Lord has a people upon the earth anywhere and ministers who are authorized to preach the gospel, he will send one to us."

Very soon their prayers were answered. In the
spring of 1836 Elder Parley P. Pratt, an apostle of The Church
of Jesus Christ of Latter-day Saints, arrived as a missionary in
Toronto. He traveled, as the ancient apostles did, without purse or scrip, which
means without money or baggage. Elder Pratt fasted and prayed for the Spirit of the
Lord to direct him to those seeking for the truth and was led to John and Leonora Taylor.
These two began to attend the meetings held by Elder Pratt.

After a short time, John asked, "Leonora, could this new religion be the answer to our
search? I am going to make a regular business of this for three weeks. I intend to follow
Brother Parley from place to place as he preaches. I am going to write down his sermons
and compare them with the scriptures. At the same time," he continued, "I will make a
careful study of the Book of Mormon and the Doctrine and Covenants, as well as the
testimony of Joseph Smith."

And that is just what he did.

John was excited to share his conclusions with Leonora: "Brother Pratt's sermons
answer my questions and make the scriptures clearer."

After this investigation he and Leonora made a decision that would change the course
of Church history. They were baptized on May 9, 1836, by Elder Parley P. Pratt.

From that moment to the end of his life, he spoke out for the Church with uncommon strength and conviction. He was fearless in facing all persecutions and difficulties. He dedicated himself to building the kingdom of God.

John immediately began to travel with Elder Pratt, preaching the gospel of Jesus Christ. He was a determined missionary. Several members of his Bible study group joined the Church. Other new converts came into the Church every day, and soon John was ordained an elder by Brother Pratt.

In the fall of 1836, when it was time for Elder Pratt to return to his home in Kirtland, Ohio, he said, "Brother Taylor, I leave the Church affairs here in Upper Canada in your charge." Although John was not quite twenty-eight years old, he said, "Brother Pratt, I will do my best to be equal to this responsibility!"

A few months later, in March of 1837, John Taylor traveled to Kirtland. He was eager to meet the Prophet Joseph Smith, and he was not disappointed. The Prophet Joseph greeted him warmly, "Brother Taylor, I welcome you with all my heart!"

John felt a thrill go through his body, for he knew he stood face-to-face with a prophet of God.

During John's visit to Kirtland he and the Prophet became good friends. John returned to Canada, and after a few months Joseph Smith and some of the Brethren traveled to Canada to meet with the Saints there. It was a glorious time for John. He told his wife: "I am grateful for this blessing. I have the daily opportunity of talking with these Brethren and listening to their instructions and the rich store of intelligence that flows continually from the Prophet Joseph."

Before Joseph Smith left Canada, he ordained John to the office of high priest. He recognized the qualities of a strong leader in John Taylor. A few months later John received a message from the Prophet asking him to join the Saints in Missouri.

John immediately answered the call. Since he and Leonora were devoted to serving the Lord in any way they could, they gave little thought to leaving their comfortable home and business in Toronto. John and a friend, an Elder Mills, obtained a covered sleigh for their families to ride in, loaded their belongings into wagons, and set out on the long and difficult trip. Elder Taylor had to stop in Indiana for a time to earn money before they could proceed to Missouri. They arrived at Far West, Missouri, about October, 1838.

Prior to the Taylors' arrival, the Prophet Joseph received a revelation calling John Taylor to be an apostle. Thus, shortly after he came to Missouri, he was ordained an apostle by Brigham Young and Heber C. Kimball. John Taylor had been a member of the Church only a little more than a year. Certainly the vision of his early youth was being fulfilled!

THINK ABOUT IT:

1. What happened to John Taylor that caused him to believe the Lord had something special for him to do in his life?
2. Tell some ways in which John Taylor showed his faithfulness and obedience in doing the Lord's work.
3. What are some of the ways that young people today can show the Lord that they will be obedient and faithful?

When John and his family arrived in Missouri in October, the Saints were suffering great persecution. Joseph Smith had been taken prisoner, and all the Saints had been ordered to leave Missouri. Thus, after his long and difficult journey from Canada, John now had to gather up his wife and family and move on to the new gathering place in

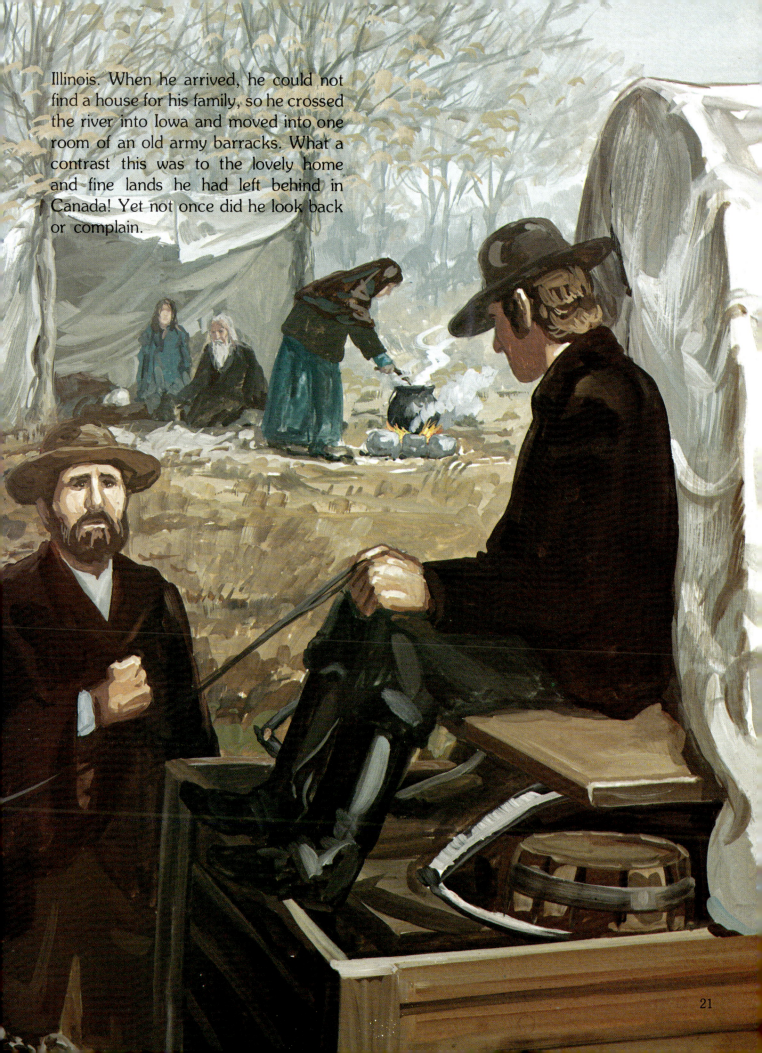

Illinois. When he arrived, he could not find a house for his family, so he crossed the river into Iowa and moved into one room of an old army barracks. What a contrast this was to the lovely home and fine lands he had left behind in Canada! Yet not once did he look back or complain.

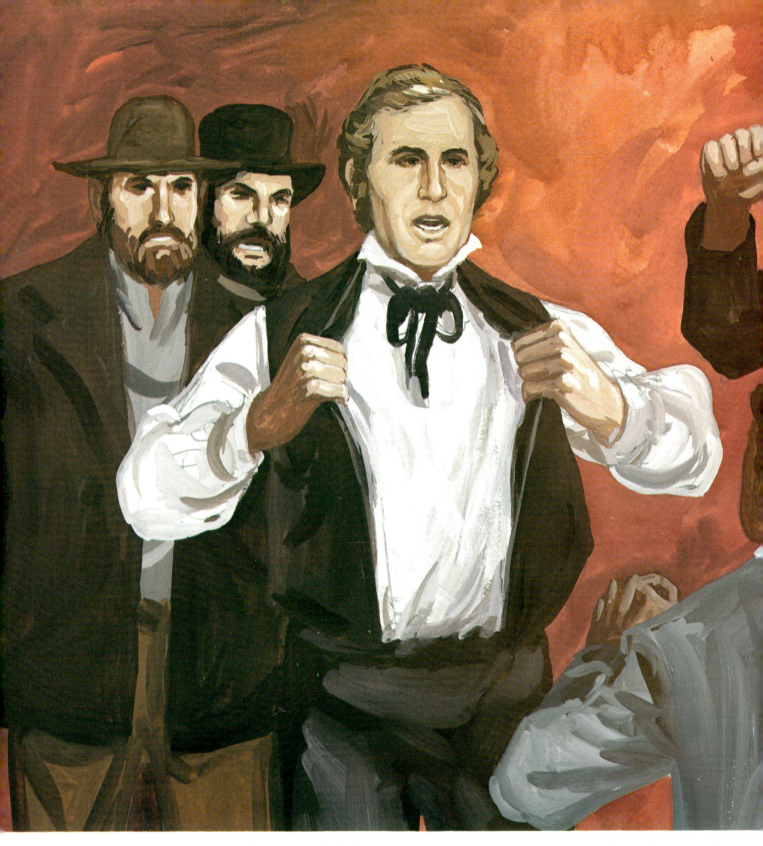

As soon as his family was settled, he began to travel in the area, preaching the gospel. John Taylor proved at once that he was willing to face any danger. He was speaking to an angry crowd at a meeting in Ohio. Among them were men who had come to tar and feather him. John knew of these evil men but stood up bold and unafraid. In a strong voice he said words like these: "I have recently come from Canada, a land ruled by a monarch. I am grateful to be in a country where the American forefathers had a great vision and gave their lives for freedom. I know that some of you intend to tar and feather me for my

religious opinions. Is this the blessing you inherited from your fathers? Is this the liberty they purchased with their hearts' blood? If so, you now have a victim. . . . " He opened his vest and stated, "Gentlemen, come on with your tar and feathers. Your victim is ready. Spirits of the patriots, gaze upon the deeds of your degenerate sons! Come on, gentlemen! Come on, I say. I am ready!" His enemies were ashamed, and not one man stepped forward.

In 1839 John was called with the other apostles to serve a mission in England. He was ill and almost penniless, yet he expressed happiness at his call. He said, "The thought of going forth at the command of God to revisit my native land, to unfold the principles of eternal truth, and to make known the things that God has revealed for the salvation of the world, overcomes every other feeling." He prayed for the protection of his wife and children and set off for England with the Brethren.

John served a splendid mission. His strong testimony and tireless efforts brought families into the Church, including the family of his wife's brother, George Cannon.

After two years John prepared to leave England. He said, "I rejoice that God has blessed my humble efforts. I have traveled 5,000 miles without purse or scrip. I have

traveled on railroads, coaches, steamboats, wagons, and on horseback. I have been amongst strangers and in strange lands, yet I have never lacked for money, clothes, friends, or a home. Neither have I ever asked a person for a farthing. Thus I have proved the Lord, and I know that he does according to his word."

The apostles left England and arrived on July 1, 1841, in Nauvoo, where hundreds of Saints had gathered to meet them. The Prophet Joseph Smith was the first to shake their hands.

Although Leonora Taylor was not well, the family was happy to be reunited. With her husband's loving care and attention, she soon regained her health.

With his missionary experience Elder Taylor became one of the most powerful writers and speakers in the Church. When the Church purchased the printing office of the *Times and Seasons* newspaper, the Prophet asked John Taylor and Wilford Woodruff to manage it.

In addition, in the fall of 1842 John also began a weekly newspaper called the *Nauvoo Neighbor*.

This was a prosperous and happy time for Elder John Taylor. He had many opportunities to serve. His publishing business was growing. People recognized his unusual wisdom and honesty, and he served on the Nauvoo City Council. He was a member of the board of regents for the Nauvoo University. He was also a colonel in the Nauvoo Legion. He wrote direct and honest articles in his newspapers and spoke with power in defense of the Church and the Prophet Joseph Smith. People began to call him "Defender of the Faith" and "Champion of Liberty."

The Prophet Joseph always enjoyed himself in the company of his friends, and he considered John to be one of his closest friends. Together they spent some happy times in Nauvoo, in spite of persecutions and problems. John Taylor had a good singing voice, and the Prophet sometimes asked John to sing for him. Joseph wrote in his journal in 1844: "A large party took a New Year's supper at my house, and had music and dancing till morning. I was in my private room with my family, Elder John Taylor, and other friends."

In the year 1844 the Prophet Joseph announced himself as a candidate for United States President. To help his cause 244 elders, including all of the Twelve Apostles except John Taylor and Willard Richards, left Nauvoo and traveled to the Eastern States to

campaign for his election. While they were away, an anti-Mormon newspaper was destroyed after publishing a vicious article against the Prophet. The enemies of the Church saw this event as a chance to destroy the Church and its leader. Joseph Smith and the Nauvoo City Council were charged with having committed a riot. A warrant was issued for their arrest. Mobs gathered.

Newspapers in nearby cities carried such headlines as "Drive Out the Mormons" and "Exterminate the Mormons." Governor Thomas Ford of Illinois traveled to Carthage and sent word to Joseph Smith to come and surrender for trial. Governor Ford promised Joseph the protection of the state of Illinois. Joseph knew that his enemies planned treachery, but he sent word that he would come.

When Joseph and Hyrum arrived, they were immediately arrested and taken to Carthage Jail. Apostles John Taylor and Willard Richards accompanied them, saying, "We will go with you, Joseph. We intend to do all we can to protect you." This was just two days before the Prophet's martyrdom.

The fatal morning of June 27, 1844, dawned clear and warm. As the prisoners looked out of the window of the upper room of Carthage Jail, they could see the wicked mobsters in the square below. During the afternoon Joseph Smith asked John to sing one of his favorite songs, "A Poor Wayfaring Man of Grief." John sang all the verses and brought some comfort to the Prophet.

Shortly after five o'clock Elder Taylor looked out the window. He saw a group of men with blackened faces run around the corner of the jail and enter the building. They all carried guns. These wicked men climbed the stairs and pushed against the door of the upper room.

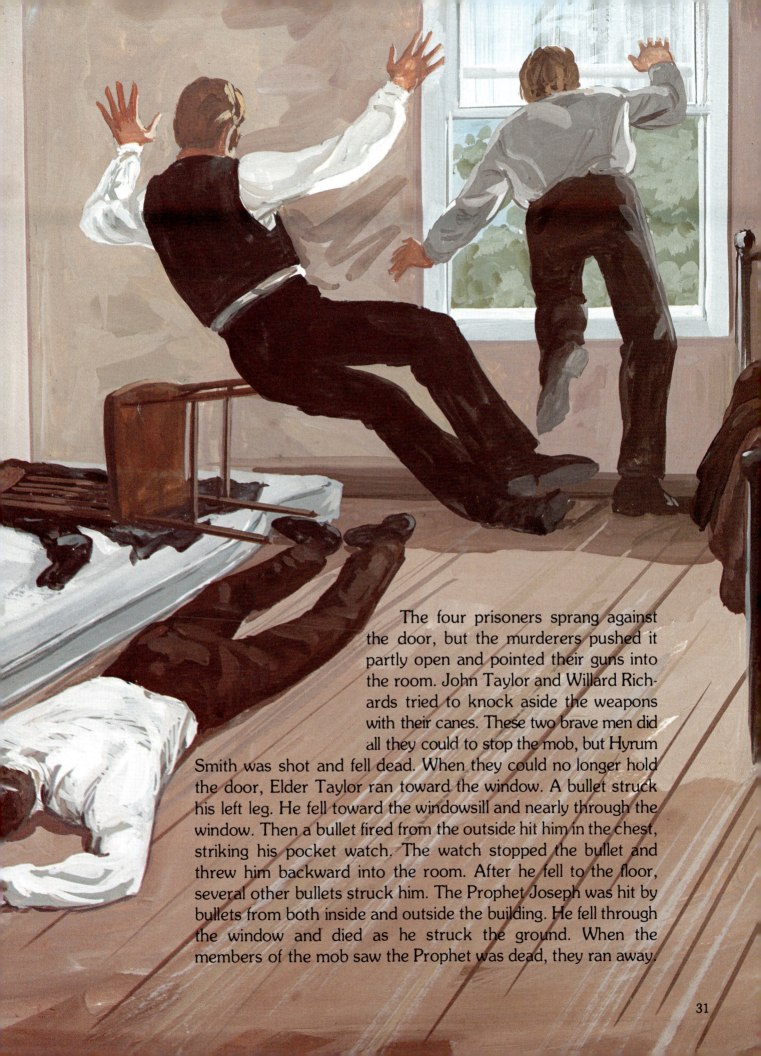

The four prisoners sprang against the door, but the murderers pushed it partly open and pointed their guns into the room. John Taylor and Willard Richards tried to knock aside the weapons with their canes. These two brave men did all they could to stop the mob, but Hyrum Smith was shot and fell dead. When they could no longer hold the door, Elder Taylor ran toward the window. A bullet struck his left leg. He fell toward the windowsill and nearly through the window. Then a bullet fired from the outside hit him in the chest, striking his pocket watch. The watch stopped the bullet and threw him backward into the room. After he fell to the floor, several other bullets struck him. The Prophet Joseph was hit by bullets from both inside and outside the building. He fell through the window and died as he struck the ground. When the members of the mob saw the Prophet was dead, they ran away.

31

Miraculously, Willard Richards was unharmed. He dragged a mattress and laid it over the wounded John Taylor. Brother Richards said, "John, this is hard to lay on you, but if your wounds are not fatal, I want you to live to tell the story. Now I will hurry for help."

Elder Richards was able to find help and to send word of the assassination to Nauvoo. Friends came and took Elder Taylor to his home in Nauvoo, where he lay ill for many weeks. During his recovery the apostles came to his home for their meetings until his wounds healed.

THINK ABOUT IT:

1. What are some of the things John Taylor did that helped the Church grow stronger?
2. Tell about some of the times when John Taylor showed his great courage.
3. How did John Taylor prove his friendship and love for the Prophet Joseph Smith?
4. How can members of the Church today show courage in standing up for what they believe?

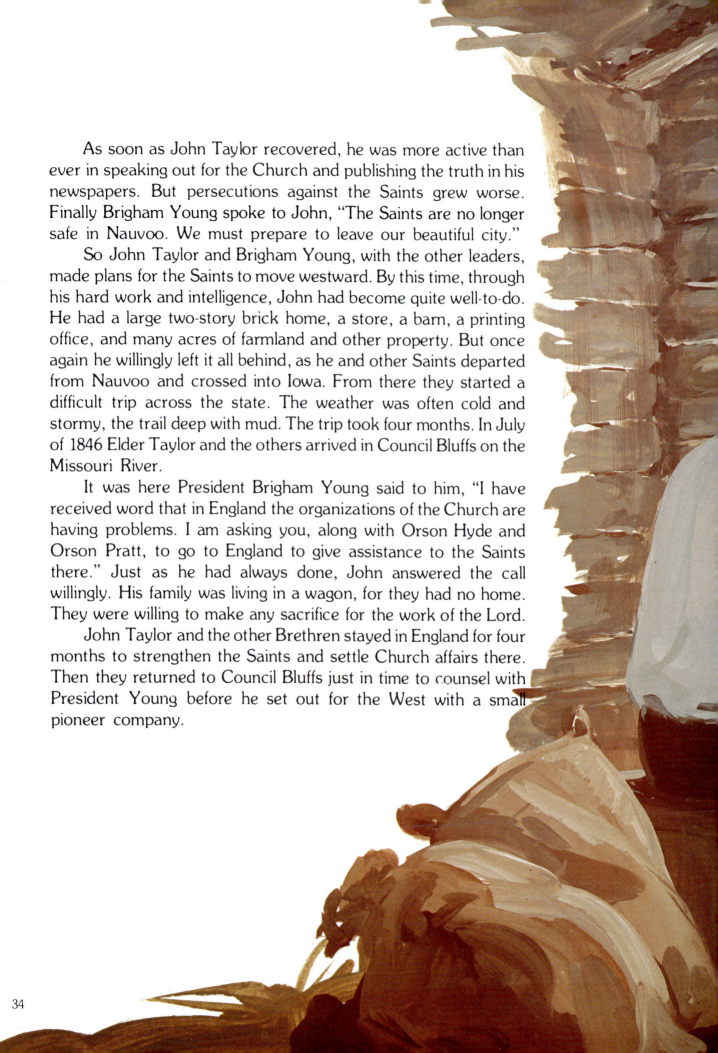

As soon as John Taylor recovered, he was more active than ever in speaking out for the Church and publishing the truth in his newspapers. But persecutions against the Saints grew worse. Finally Brigham Young spoke to John, "The Saints are no longer safe in Nauvoo. We must prepare to leave our beautiful city."

So John Taylor and Brigham Young, with the other leaders, made plans for the Saints to move westward. By this time, through his hard work and intelligence, John had become quite well-to-do. He had a large two-story brick home, a store, a barn, a printing office, and many acres of farmland and other property. But once again he willingly left it all behind, as he and other Saints departed from Nauvoo and crossed into Iowa. From there they started a difficult trip across the state. The weather was often cold and stormy, the trail deep with mud. The trip took four months. In July of 1846 Elder Taylor and the others arrived in Council Bluffs on the Missouri River.

It was here President Brigham Young said to him, "I have received word that in England the organizations of the Church are having problems. I am asking you, along with Orson Hyde and Orson Pratt, to go to England to give assistance to the Saints there." Just as he had always done, John answered the call willingly. His family was living in a wagon, for they had no home. They were willing to make any sacrifice for the work of the Lord.

John Taylor and the other Brethren stayed in England for four months to strengthen the Saints and settle Church affairs there. Then they returned to Council Bluffs just in time to counsel with President Young before he set out for the West with a small pioneer company.

Before he left, Brigham Young said, "John, will you take the responsibility for the Saints who remain here at Winter Quarters? Organize them into groups and help them prepare to follow later." Faithful Elder Taylor set to work immediately, and by late June his party was ready to begin the 1000-mile journey to the West. There were 1,533 people, 600 wagons, 124 horses, and 887 cows. Just imagine the movement of such a large group of people with their belongings and animals. They must have stretched out for miles, as they journeyed slowly across the plains!

When John Taylor's company arrived in western Wyoming, they met Brigham Young and a small party who were on their way back to Winter Quarters. The weary travelers, those going east and those going west, were excited to be together. "Brother Taylor," Brigham said, "we have found a permanent gathering place for the Saints in the Great Salt Lake Valley!"

John Taylor asked the women to prepare a special dinner for President Young and his company, and the women quickly went to work. They set up tables of whatever pieces of wood or furniture they could gather together and covered them with the lovely white cloths they were carrying across the plains to add beauty to their rough homes. After the happy preparations, the travelers all sat down to a royal "feast in the wilderness!" There was roasted meat, wild game, and even some fish. Pickles, relishes, fruits, and jellies saved for special occasions were set on the tables. There was laughter and happy talk. After dinner President Brigham Young called out, "Let us have music and dancing!" The fiddles played; the crowd danced quadrilles and Scottish reels. It was a day that would live in the memories of the pioneers!

The following morning the two companies parted. Brigham Young went eastward. John Taylor continued westward to the Salt Lake Valley, arriving on the afternoon of October 5, 1847.

The first year in the valley was very difficult for the pioneers, even though they worked as hard as they could. In the spring of 1848 they planted many acres of wheat and other crops. Then one summer day, just as their wheat was beginning to ripen, a terrible thing happened! First, the people noticed a few ugly black crickets hopping and flying into their fields. Then more and more came, until finally there were thousands. The crickets began to eat the ripening crops! The people were frightened and joined together to battle this new enemy. They knocked the crickets off the wheat stalks and stomped on them, but still the crickets came. The people did not stop working from sunrise to sunset. When the sun went down, the crickets hid, but as soon as the sun came up, they poured out and landed again on the crops. The people were helpless against the black horde, and they knew they could not survive the winter if the crickets ate their crops. The leaders called for a special day of fasting and prayer to plead for the Lord's help. Elder John Taylor added his mighty prayers to those of the other Saints.

Finally in midafternoon a sharp cry was heard! The people looked up and saw a great cloud coming toward them. "What is it?" one man cried. "What can it be?" asked others. Then someone shouted, "It's a flock of seagulls!" And that's just what it was! The flock was so large that it almost blocked out the sun when it flew over the people. The gulls settled down on the fields. "They are eating the crickets," shouted a woman. The people began to weep and laugh and praise the Lord. They cried, "It's a miracle! The Lord has answered our prayers!"

The gulls returned day after day until the crickets were gone. A large amount of the harvest had been destroyed, but the pioneers were able to harvest enough to keep from starving during the next winter.

All during this time Elder Taylor showed strong, faithful leadership. One historian said, "Many leaned on Elder Taylor's strength in those days. When despair settled over the colony, he gave them hope; when the weak faltered, he strengthened them; those cast down with sorrow, he comforted and cheered."

John Taylor was called on two more missions—one to France and one to the Eastern States. As always Elder Taylor was fearless and diligent in the work he was called to do. During his mission to the Eastern States he published a paper called *The Mormon* to explain the doctrines of the Church to nonmembers there.

John returned to Utah during the time when the United States had sent Johnston's army to put down the so-called rebellion of the Saints. In response to this threat, Elder Taylor gave a powerful speech in the Tabernacle. "What would be your feelings," he asked the congregation, "if the United States wanted to drive us from our own homes? All you that are willing to set fire to your property and lay it in ashes rather than submit to their military rule, manifest it by raising your hands!" Four thousand of the Saints raised their hands in a unanimous vote. Fortunately the crisis passed, and the Saints did not have to burn their homes.

John Taylor, as President of the Quorum of the Twelve Apostles, became responsible for the affairs of the Church when President Brigham Young died in August of 1877. In 1880, at October conference, John Taylor was sustained President of The Church of Jesus Christ of Latter-day Saints. He proved to be a strong and active leader. He pushed the Church forward in temple completions, in the organization of stakes and wards, and in missionary work.

The leaders of the Church came under much persecution at this time because of the practice of plural marriage. The federal government had passed laws against plural marriage, but the Church leaders were honorable men and would not leave their plural families. John Taylor was one of these leaders. He finally went into retirement to escape those who tried to arrest him, but he continued to send messages to direct the

affairs of the Church. He also sent letters to his wives and children to counsel them and express his love for them. In a letter to his family he wrote, "I feel to bless and praise God's holy name. I . . . acknowledge His hand in all things, and I am very anxious that you should do the same. For to the Lord we are indebted for every blessing we enjoy in this life, and the life which is to come."

President Taylor's health began to fail in the summer of 1887. He died peacefully on July 25, 1887, in Kaysville, Utah. The Saints deeply mourned his passing. The Brethren wrote of him, "He never knew the feeling of fear connected with the work of God . . . even when his life was threatened, his knees never trembled, his hand never shook."

This great prophet and president was outstanding in many ways—in integrity, honesty, and courage, in love, loyalty, and wisdom, in justice and kindness. The Saints in the early days admired and loved him for his great qualities. The Saints of today could well follow the example of President John Taylor.

The vision of his youth was fulfilled. The Lord had indeed something special for John Taylor to do.

TESTIMONY

We are engaged in a great work . . . a work that has been spoken of by all the holy prophets since the world was; namely, the dispensation of the fullness of times wherein God will gather together all things in one, whether they be things in the earth, or things in the heavens; and for this purpose God revealed Himself, as also the Lord Jesus Christ, unto His servant the Prophet Joseph Smith, when the Father pointed to the Son and said: "This is my beloved Son, in whom I am well pleased, hear ye Him." He further restored the everlasting gospel; together with the Aaronic and Melchizedek Priesthoods; both of which are everlasting as God is. . . . I believe in God, in Jesus Christ, and in the exaltation of the human family, and consequently have acted and do act in accordance with that belief. . . . I believe in a religion that I can live for, or die for. . . . I would rather trust in the living God than in any other power on earth. . . . I would rather have God for my friend than all other influences and powers outside. (Quoted from Roberts, *Life of John Taylor,* pp. 394, 422-23.)